D1063535

LET'S LEARN
ABOUT
KOREA

CUSTOMS OF KOREA 예절과 풍습

Revised edition

LET'S LEARN ABOUT KOREA

Revised edition

CUSTOMS OF KOREA 예절과 풍습

Text by Suzanne Crowder Han   Illustrated by Lee Gi-eun

Hollym

LET'S LEARN ABOUT KOREA

Copyright © 1992
by Hollym Corp., Publishers

All rights reserved.

First published in 1992
Revised edition, 2009
Second printing, 2013
by Hollym International Corp., USA
Phone 908 353 1655   **Fax** 908 353 0255
http://www.hollym.com   **e-Mail** contact@hollym.com

 Hollym

Published simultaneously in Korea
by Hollym Corp., Publishers, Seoul, Korea
Phone +82 2 734 5087   **Fax** +82 2 730 5149
http://www.hollym.co.kr   **e-Mail** info@hollym.co.kr

ISBN : 978-1-56591-290-8

Printed in Korea

Note to Parents

Since ancient times, Koreans have placed great emphasis on courtesy, especially respect for elders, and have adhered to strict rules of proper and correct behavior. These rules have always been taught within the home as one's behavior and appearance are considered a reflection of one's family.

The aim of this book is thus twofold: to introduce Korean customs and to introduce some of the ideas and values Korean children are taught. The information is presented through the eyes of a young Korean girl as she goes about her daily life.

한국사람들은 오래 전부터 단정한 품행과 사람들 사이에 지켜야 할 예의를 중시하며 살아왔습니다. 특히, 조상과 웃어른에 대한 예절을 가장 중요하게 여겼습니다. 한 사람의 태도는 그 집안의 됨됨이를 말해 주기 때문에 가정에서의 교육이 엄격했습니다.

이 책은 한국의 가정에서 치루어야 할 행사와 지켜야 할 몇 가지의 예절을 이해하기 쉽게 풀이한 그림책입니다.

아기를 낳게 해 달라고 삼신할머니께 기도를 드립니다.

어머니께서는 물 맑고 아름다운 산천을 찾아
떠나셨습니다. 삼신할머니께 정성 드려 기도하면 아들을
낳을 수 있다고 어머니는 믿고 계셨습니다.
　삼신할머니는 아기들을 세상에 태어나게 해 준다는
세 신령을 말합니다.

　'나도 남동생이 태어났으면 좋겠습니다.'

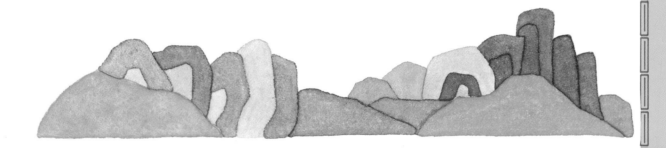

Mother has gone to a lovely spot beside a stream deep in
the mountains to pray in front of an auspicious looking rock
to the Samsin Halmeoni, or Birth Grandmother, to bless her
with a child. Samsin refers to three (*sam*) spirits (*sin*) which
are believed to govern the birth of a child and its growth.
　I would like to have a baby brother.

Praying to the Birth Grandmother for a baby

아기가 태어났습니다.

옛날에는 대문 앞에 금줄을 걸어 바깥의 부정과 출입을 막았습니다.

마침내 남동생이 태어났습니다. 아버지께서 대문 앞에
금줄을 쳐 두셨습니다. 집안에 갓난아기가 있기 때문에
여러 가지로 조심해야 한다고 하십니다. 금줄을 치는 것은
한국의 풍습으로, 출입을 금지한다는 신호입니다.
　사내아기가 태어나면 새끼줄에 붉은 고추와 숯을 끼우고
여자아기가 태어나면 고추 대신 청솔가지 또는 종이를
꽂아 둔다고 합니다.

'아기야, 건강하게 어서어서 자라라.'

Father hung a special straw rope across the gate to warn
people not to enter because there is a newborn baby in the
house. He told me that people carry germs, so it is best for
outsiders to stay away until our baby becomes strong. The red
peppers show that our baby is a boy. If it were a girl, there
would be pieces of paper instead of peppers.
　I hope my brother grows big and strong.

**"A newborn in residence" is what the straw rope across
the gate indicates.**

아기가 태어나서 처음 맞이하는 생일날, 돌잔치를 합니다.

오늘은 내 동생이 태어나 처음 맞이하는 생일입니다.
친척과 이웃 사람들이 많이 오셨습니다. 어머니께서는
맛있는 음식으로 가득 찬 돌상을 차리셨습니다. 그리고
쌀·돈·실·책·붓도 올려놓았습니다.
  한국에서는 돌날, 아기의 장래를 알아보는 풍습이
있습니다. 상 위에서 아기가 맨 처음 쌀이나 돈을
잡으면 커서 부자가 되고, 실을 잡으면 오래 살며,
책·붓을 잡으면 공부를 잘할 것이라고 생각하였습니다.

  '내 동생은 자라서 무엇이 될까?'

Today is my brother's first birthday. Many relatives and
neighbors have come to help us celebrate. Mother has
prepared all kinds of good food for our guests. The highlight
of our celebration is when my brother, dressed in a colorful
costume, is put before a table of special foods and objects such
as uncooked rice, skeins of thread, writing brushes and money.
Koreans believe that what the child picks up first foretells his
future: for example, if he picks up money or rice, he will be
wealthy; if he picks up thread, he will live long; if he picks up
a writing brush or book, he will be studious.
  I wonder what my brother will be?

It's baby's first birthday.

"새해 복 많이 받으세요." 설날 아침, 웃어른께 세배를 드립니다.

음력 1월 1일.

오늘은 즐거운 설날입니다.

아침 일찍 일어나 설빔으로 예쁘게 단장을 합니다.

차례를 지냅니다.

할아버지 할머니께 세배를 드립니다.

"할아버지 할머니, 새해 복 많이 받으세요."

아버지 어머니께도 세배를 드립니다.

"아버지 어머니, 새해 복 많이 받으세요."

할아버지 할머니께서 우리들에게 공부를 잘 하라고
말씀하셨습니다.

It is Lunar New Year's Day. My brother and I are dressed in our new traditional Korean outfits called *hanbok*. The memorial offering to ancestors is over and it is time for us to do our New Year's bows, or *sebae*. First we bow to Grandfather and Grandmother and offer our New Year's greetings and then we do the same to Father and Mother.

Grandfather and Grandmother tell us to study hard.

"May you have good fortune throughout the year."

"안녕하세요?" 웃어른을 만나면 공손히 인사를 합니다.

우리 집에는 오래전부터 내려오는 가훈이 있습니다.
할아버지 할머니께서는, 아버지 어머니한테
예의범절을 가르쳐 주셨습니다.
아버지 어머니께서는, 우리들에게 예절 바른 사람이
되라고 말씀하십니다.

"할아버지, 안녕하세요."
이웃집 어른을 만나면 언제나 공손히 인사를 합니다.

My family has a motto that has come down to us through
the ages. It is: "Always be polite." My parents are always telling
my brother and me to be courteous to others, especially older
people. They are teaching us the same manners and rules of
behavior they learned from their parents.

I must greet friends and neighbors whenever I meet them.

"How are you?" Mother and I greet an elderly man on
the street.

"안녕히 가세요." 손님이 가실 때는 대문 밖에서 배웅을 합니다.

우리 집에 손님이 오셨습니다.
"아저씨, 안녕하세요?"
방 안에서 나와 인사로 맞이합니다.

손님이 가십니다.
"아저씨, 안녕히 가세요."
대문 밖에서 배웅을 합니다.

When a visitor comes to our house, I must come out of my room to say hello. And, when the visitor leaves, I must come out of my room to say farewell. I go outside to the gate with my parents to see him off. Not seeing a guest to the gate is discourteous.

"Goodbye, Mister," I say, bowing slightly the way my parents taught me.

"Goodbye," I say, bowing slightly to our guest, as my parents see him off at the gate.

가족이 모여 앉아 오손도손 밥을 먹습니다.

밥을 먹습니다.

할아버지 할머니께서 먼저 수저를 드셨습니다.

아버지 어머니께서도 밥을 잡수십니다.

나도 맛있게 밥을 먹습니다.

음식이 입 안에 있을 때에는 말을 하지 않습니다.

'수저와 젓가락을 바르게 사용했습니다.'

 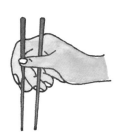  

We sit on the floor and eat at a low table. Each person has a bowl of rice and a bowl of soup but everyone eats together from the other dishes of food. We use a spoon and chopsticks to eat. No one, not even Father and Mother, eats until Grandfather and Grandmother start eating. It is a way of showing our respect for them. And, of course, no one speaks with food in their mouth.

Using chopsticks is not so difficult.

It's fun when all the family eats together.

한국에서 예로부터 전해오던 결혼식입니다.

신랑은 말을 타고 장가갑니다.
신부는 족두리를 쓰고, 연지 곤지를 찍었습니다.
마당에 차일을 치고 멍석을 깝니다.
초례상을 마주하고
신부는 신랑에게 절을 합니다.
신랑도 신부에게 절을 합니다.
신부는 가마 타고 시집갑니다.

'오늘은 좋은 날 기쁜 날,
 사촌 언니 시집가는 날입니다.'

Uncle is getting married. He and his bride are having a traditional Korean wedding. They are wearing clothes patterned after the robes that court officials and court ladies wore in ancient times. As in olden times, the ceremony is being held outdoors. The bride and groom bow to each other, exchange cups of wine, bow to each other again, and then bow to the guests, which marks the completion of the wedding and the beginning of a feast for everyone. In ancient times, Uncle would have ridden on a horse to his bride's house for the marriage ceremony and then taken her home in a special carrier called palanquin.

Traditional weddings are fun and colorful.

A traditional Korean wedding ceremony

태어나서 60번째 맞이하는 생일을 '환갑'이라 하며 장수 잔치를 합니다.

할아버지께서 60번째로 맞이하시는 생신날입니다.

아버지 어머니께서 장수 잔치를 베풀어 드립니다.

사람은 일생 동안 여러 가지 궂은 일, 좋은 일, 슬픈 일,

즐거운 일을 겪으면서 살아갑니다.

오늘은, 할아버지 할머니께서 희로애락을 함께

나누었던, 많은 사람들과 지난날을 다시 회상하며

장수를 축하받는 뜻 깊은 날입니다.

'할아버지 할머니, 오래오래 사세요.'

Mother and Father have prepared a large feast to celebrate Grandfather's *hwan-gap*, or sixtieth birthday. All of our relatives and many neighbors have come to honor him with bows and cups of wine. It is a special day for it marks his completion of a full cycle of the sixty year Oriental zodiac. In the past, before modern medicine, few people lived that long so it was considered a great accomplishment.

I bow to my grandparents and say, "May you live a long life."

It is Grandfather's sixtieth birthday, a very special birthday for Koreans.

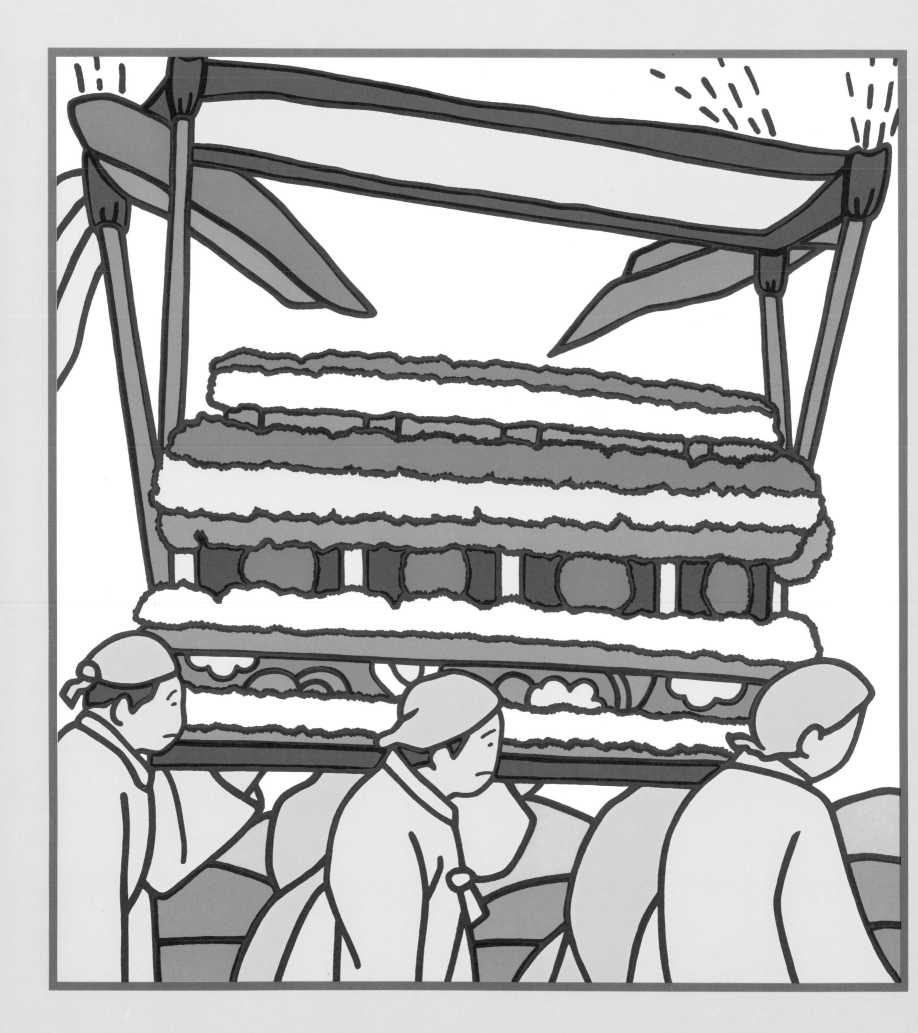

돌아가신 분을 장사 지냅니다.

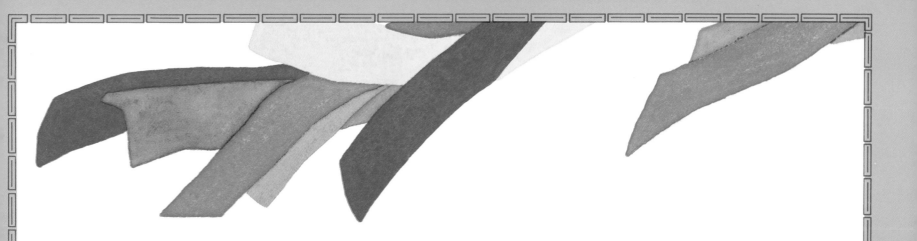

슬픈 날입니다.

할아버지께서 돌아가셨습니다.

아침에 해가 뜨고 저녁에 다시 지듯이,

사람도 태어나서 언젠가는 떠나게 됩니다.

화려하게 장식한 꽃상여 속에 할아버지께서 누워 계십니다.

상여꾼들은 슬픈 노래를 부르며 상여를 메고 무덤을

향해 떠납니다.

'슬펐습니다.'

It is a sad day because Grandfather has died. He now lies
in a coffin inside the colorful bier which is being carried to a
grave high up the mountainside. The men sing sad songs as
they carry the bier on their shoulders. My family and I walk
behind them, thinking about Grandfather and wailing.
    What a sad day.

A funeral procession

부모님 돌아가신 날을 기일로 하여 1년에 한 번씩 제사를 지냅니다.

할아버지의 제삿날입니다.
돌아가신 할아버지의 영혼이 해마다 오늘,
찾아오신다고 합니다.
단정한 몸가짐과 경건한 마음으로 할아버지의 모습을
다시 한번 기억해 봅니다.

'보고 싶은 할아버지…….'

It is the anniversary of Grandfather's death so the family pays homage to him with Confucian rites. All the men and boys bow and offer food and wine to his spirit. Then we all share the food and talk about Grandfather and other ancestors.
I miss my Grandfather, especially when we hold the memorial rites for him.

Memorial rites for Grandfather

명절날, 조상의 산소를 찾아가서 성묘를 합니다.

음력 8월 15일.
추석이 왔습니다.
모두가 고향을 찾아갑니다.
할아버지 할머니의 산소에 가서 잔디를 가꾸고
잡초도 뽑았습니다.
햇곡식으로 빚은 송편과 햇과일을 할아버지 할머니께
먼저 드립니다.

그리고
절을 하였습니다.

On festive days such as New Year's and Chuseok, or the
Harvest Moon Day, Koreans visit the graves of their ancestors.
My family visits Grandfather's grave. We weed and trim the grass
on the grave and offer special foods to his spirit.
    Then we all bow together to show our respect.

Venerating our ancestors

Let's Color the Picture!